C ᶜ ˢ

B

WITH NATHAN

A

Copyright:

ABCs
WITH NATHAN

Dedication:

Thank you to my handsome inspiration, Nathan. Your smile and rumbunctious nature have blessed me so much. I wanted to share your fun personality with others because there is a fun way to learn the ABCs, especially if you are a part of it.

We wanted to write a book that is especially dedicated to young boys. This book is funny, and yes, the ABCs are in here. Turn the pages and enjoy the fun, laughs, and boy moments to make any parent smile.

Special thanks to all of my children; I love you all. To my husband, thank you.

I am excited to work on a book with my son Nathan. He helped me to come up with a very special way of teaching you the alphabet.

Are you ready to travel through the alphabet with us?

Ayden is my brother, and he is **awesome**! I would say **amazing**! He likes **apples**, **astronauts**, **and** the continent of **Africa**! **After** I wrote this, I remembered that I rode in **an airplane and** went to the **airport!**

Boys are the **best!** My nickname is **Bean,** and my brother's is **Bayden.** I like **balls, brownies,** and **Brazil.** My stepdad tells me he is taking me to the jungle! I **bet** I will see a **BIG** snake or spider!

Bad

Busted

Booger

BINGO

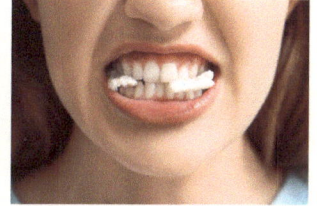

I have a dog named **China.** She is black and brown with long hair. She **chews** up everything and lowers her ears when my mom **calls** her name. She likes **carrots,** her **crate**, and going for a **cruise** in the **car** with the windows down.

Darren is the name my **dad** calls me. I **do** like the name. I also like **ducks**, **donuts**, and **dancing**. How about you? **Did** I tell you I can **drive**? My mom said I was good to be four.

Every time my mom makes **eggs** for breakfast I always say, "no thanks." Are there foods you don't like to **eat**? I like **elderberries**, **elbow** macaroni, and **egg** rolls. I also love cake! Hey, it **ends** with the letter **e**!

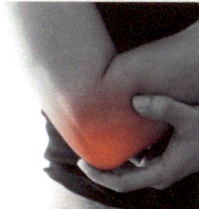

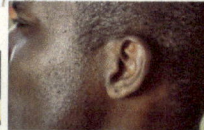

Fresh

Fangs

My grandmother has a lot of **fish!** Her **fish** sometimes **fight** for space and control of the tank. My grandmother's house has **frogs, frosted** windows, and a **fence** outside. Grandma will always turn on the water hose and spray us when it is hot outside.

FLAVOR

F❤RGIVE

Fashion

Fart

Frozen

When I do well, my mom always tells me, **"Good job!"** I love it when I do **great**, and she smiles at me. My mom likes **grapes, going** to the backyard with us, and **gorillas**! I like **grapes**, but the ones with the seeds can be annoying unless you spit the seeds at your brother!

Have you ever **had** a ghost pepper? They are very **hot** and can make you cry. When your mouth is **hot**, you might **hop** on one foot, **hold** your **head**, or even go to the **hospital.** I don't like spicy foods, I leave that to my dad. **He** loves **hot** wings!

  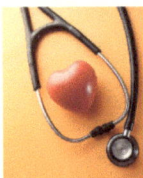   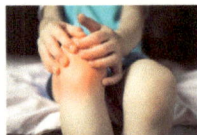

   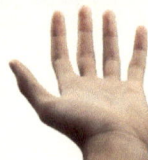

Now, I love ice cream. **It is** tasty and has many flavors. **Ice** cream **is icy**, can **instantly** freeze your tongue, and gets sticky and **icky** when **it** melts. Try to eat **it** fast but not too fast, or you can get a brain freeze—and yup, **it** hurts a little, but not for long.

Idea

Insect

Icey
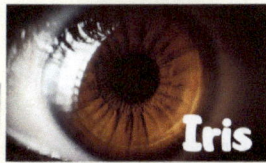
Iris

Ion

Ignore

Ink

Immortal

ILLEGAL

iSSUE 13

My older brother is named **Joshua**. He grew up playing sports and likes a lot of things with the letter "**j**." Like **jumping**, **jigsaw** puzzles, and **justice.** Do you know if a lawyer is in your family? Or have you heard of that song that says, "Hit the road, **Jack**?" I love that part when it says, "What you say!"

Jerry Curl

Jumbo

Judo

Flying a **kite** is something I have not done yet, but I plan to! The weather outside has to be  windy for it to work the best. Other things outside that start with the letter **"K'** are **kangaroos**, **kings** who rule a **kingdom**, and sour **kumquats** that grow on trees. I tried one once and politely said, "Hmm, you can have this back, Mom." She laughed and smiled at me.

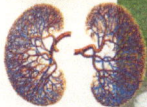    

15

Nathan's favorite animal is the **lion**. He **likes** how the **lion** roars and **licks** up water to drink. The animal is so strong. Other animals he **likes** with the letter "l" are **leopards**, **lizards**, and **lamas**! He **loves** how the **lama** spits at people and **laughs** when he sees it. But don't spit on anyone; it is rude for humans to do that.

Monsters are not real, but sometimes it can feel like they are. To **make** sure Nathan doesn't get scared, he never watches **movies with** scary creatures or **music**. What are some things that scare you that start with the letter **m**? Having to eat **mushrooms**, **mushy** peas, or **mashed** potatoes? Oh, do you want to see my **muscles**?

Muscles

Music

mirror

    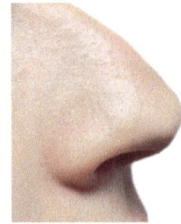

No one likes to eat **nasty** food. But some foods you need to eat are **nutritious**. What are some healthy things you like to eat? Do you like **nectarines**, **nutmeg**, or **nuts**? My mom gives me vitamins, so I eat enough fruits and vegetables; she says I need to eat them to grow big and strong!

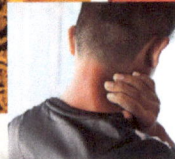

October

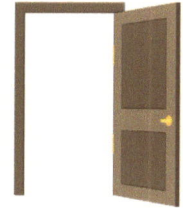

Other things you can like are **occupations**. These are jobs. Can you think of some jobs starting with the letter "**o**"? Do you know an **optometrist**, **oceanographer**, or an **oil** driller? I love to dig like my dog in the backyard. I haven't found gold or **oil**, but it never hurts to try; plus it is fun!

Peanuts are a food children shouldn't eat if they have allergies. Nuts can be healthy, but not if you have an allergy. Here are a few other things that start with the letter "**p**." Have you heard of **police** officers, **post** office workers, or **photographers**. Do you like to take **pictures**?

Parent

Did you know there are **queens** in certain parts of the world? The **queen** has responsibilities to take care of her people. I know most of them like **quilts**, the **quiet** to think, and answering difficult **questions**. I call my mom **queen** all the time. Do you think your mom is a **queen**? You will after reading A *Kiss From Yah*!

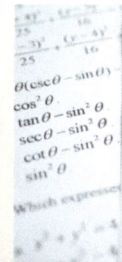

quantum

quad

quantity

NEVER QUIT!

Have you ever seen a **rabbit**? My older sister Zoe is allergic to furry bunnies. She really likes  them and would love to have them as a pet, though. I meant to ask, are there things you are allergic to? Like **rats**, **raisins**, or **roses**? Be careful with **roses**; they have thorns that can poke you.

Relax

Roger

Silly

Have you ever **started** running to win a race but **stopped**? **Sometimes**, when you **start** a race, you want to quit. If you keep running, you might surprise yourself and win! **Stay** encouraged! Other words with the letter "**s**" you want to know are **super**, **strong**, and **special**. I remember when I **started** using my **scooter**, I fell off a lot, before I got it.

  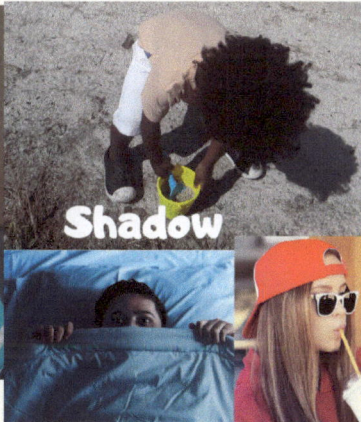  

Sleep

Shadow

Swimming

23

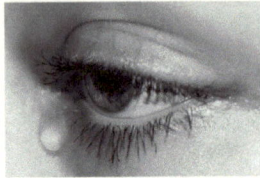   

Kayda, my older sister, had a pet **turtle** a few years ago. She loved it but decided to let it go when it got **too** big to keep in a **tank**. She misses **the turtle** still, but is glad it's free in **the** wild **to** make friends. What kind of a pet would you like **to** have? Do you **think** you would like a **tarantula**, **tiger**, or **toucan**? A **talking** bird who knew **they** could be so cool.

Towels

Tongue

Traveling

Turf

Tight

My sister and a lot of girls I know like **unicorns**. I don't see what the big deal is when a horse has a horn; girls. Now, what I like is a monkey walking on a tightrope with an **umbrella**! Do you like things that start with the letter "**u**"? How about super **underwear**, **umpires**, or the **universe**? I like to look **up** at the stars when I lie down in the grass in my backyard. Do you?

vehicles

I want to visit **Venezuela** and go to the beach! I want to make sand castles, be in the sun, and play in the water. What are some things you can think to do in a sunny place? You can ride in a tourist **van**, **visit** restaurants near your hotel, or go **virtually** anywhere with your imagination. If you haven't traveled on a **vacation** yet, try to go in your mind. There are so many places to see!

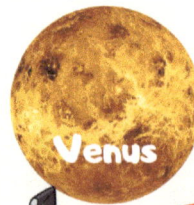

Victory

Venus

Vision

VOTE

Nathan drinks at least 5 to 6 glasses of **water** each day. Do you know how important it is to have **water**? Some creatures cannot live long **without water**. Like a **whale**, **walrus**, and **white** shark! Can you think of other animals that start **with** the letter "w"?

War

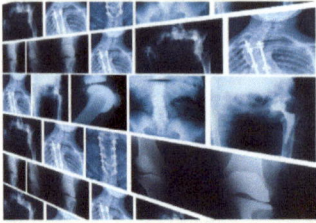  

When three of my siblings were young, they had to get an **X-ray**. They each needed casts because they had a bone fracture! While they were healing, I played the **xylophone** for them, my mom gave them a bo**x** of candies, and we read a book with a fo**x**, Sparkle's Sweet Goodbye. I couldn't think of too many words with the letter "**x**". Can you?

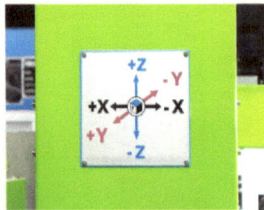

X-Ray Fish

XENOPS

Yes, the letter "**y**" is included in my sister's favorite color. Do you know what it is? **Yellow**! Zoe loves the color **yellow**. I'm not sure if it is because the sun is **yellow**. What things can you think of that start with the letter "**y**?" How about a **yawn**, **youngest**, or **yours**? I am the **youngest,** and everything is mine.

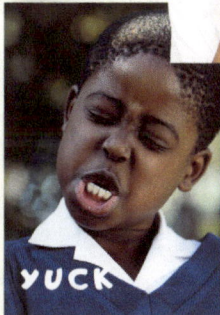

ZOO KEEPER

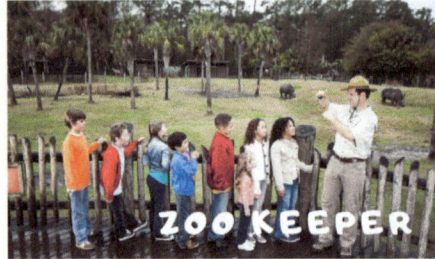

The last letter is the best one, "**z**"! How many words can you think of that start with the letter "**z**"? Did you say **zipline**, **zipper**, and **zoo**? I **zip** up my coat every winter before I go out the door. I want to **zipline** in the jungle one day, and we plan to go to the **zoo** this summer! Maybe I will see you there! I will likely be by the lions, **zebras**, or the gorilla.

Z

ZOO

Activity

Can you tell me which page the Astronaut is on? Where does he/she work?

Can you find a giraffe? Where do they live?

Where are a dozen eggs found in your house?
Do you know what animal lays the eggs spoken about in this book?

How old are you?

Do you remember my favorite animal? What letter does it start with?

Can you name something that starts with the letter "m"?

What's your favorite color? What letter does it start with?

More Fun

What can you do outside in your backyard?

What letter does your sister's, brother's, father's, or mother's name start with?

What country do you want to visit?

What do you want to do on vacation?

Can you draw your favorite food?

What is your favorite animal sound? Try making the sound. Can you roar like a lion?

Can you name something that starts with a "w"?

What piece of money starts with the letter "q"?

Great Job!

I want to tell you that you did amazing work completing this book. Keep reading the book so you can recognize the letters and sounds that make up the words and names for the pictures you have seen.

The best way to start reading is for you to continue to hear your parents, friends, siblings, or even your own voice read to you.

I would love to read this book to you, but I am still learning to read at the moment myself. So, if you scan the QR code, my Mom and I will read it together.

Dr. Lee has authored over twenty books across more than seven genres: adult, children, youth fiction, self-help, spiritual growth, novels, business, and empowerment to help people in their most profound times of need.

She is also passionate about coaching programs WAE Process (Write Anything Easily), Embrace Your Crown, Turn Key Solution for Small and New Businesses, and The Lesson for Youth and Teenagers.

- Connect with me using the QR or visit
- AuthorKLee.com
- Social sites with the handle: AuthorKLee

Get Published with KLE Publishing!

If you need a ghostwriter, editor, or want to publish a book visit
KLEPub.com or call 770-240-0089 Ext. 1

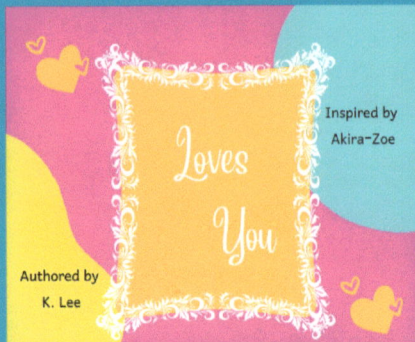

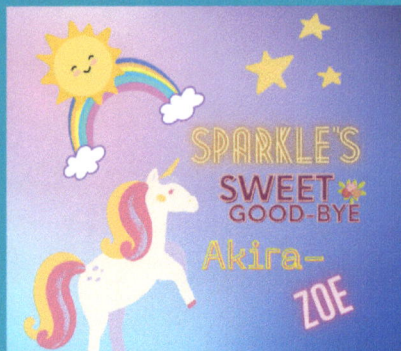

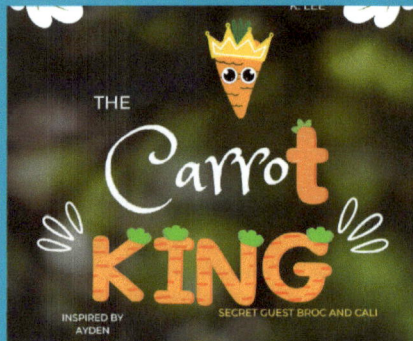

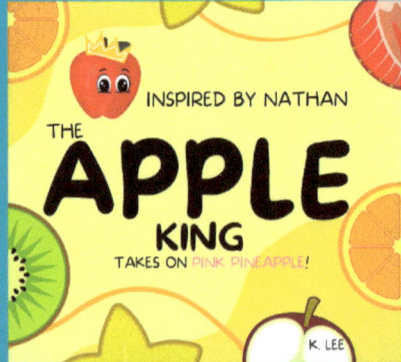

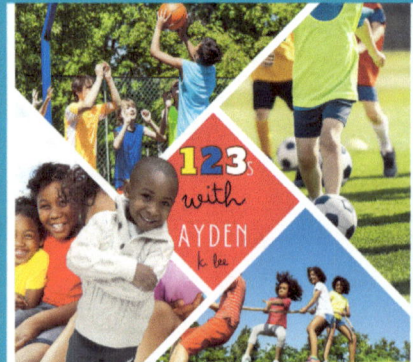

Loves You

Inspired by
Akira-Zoe

Authored by
K. Lee

SPARKLE'S SWEET GOOD-BYE

Akira-ZOE

WITH NATHAN
A B Cs

K. LEE

Let's Get Social

by K. Lee

MOM

Authored and illustrated by
Nakieta Calhoun

THE Carrot KING

INSPIRED BY
AYDEN

SECRET GUEST BROC AND CALI

The Love Jar

By
K. Lee

INSPIRED BY NATHAN

THE APPLE KING

TAKES ON PINK PINEAPPLE!

K. LEE

123 with AYDEN
k. lee

Order More Books Today!

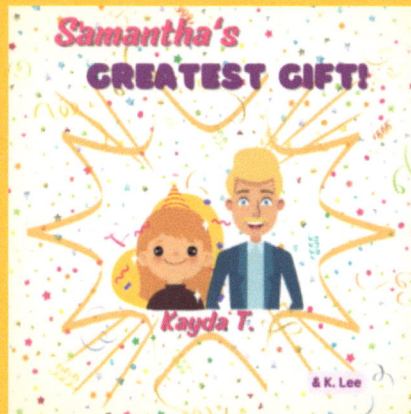

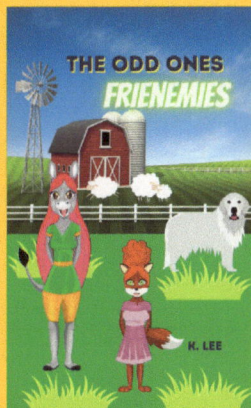

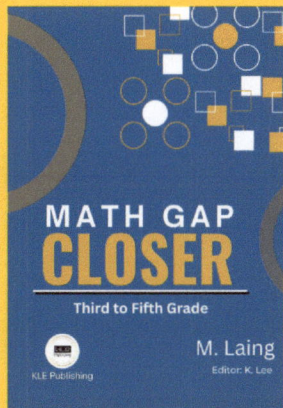

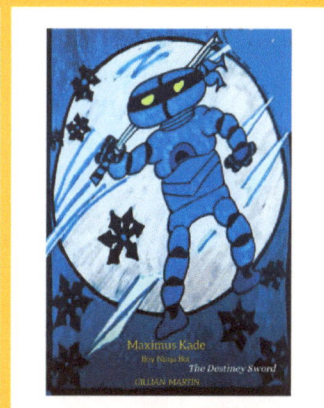

If you need a ghostwriter, editor, or want to publish a book visit KLEPub.com or call 770-240-0089 Ext. 1

www.ingramcontent.com/pod-product-compliance
Lightning Source LLC
Chambersburg PA
CBHW061143030426
42335CB00002B/85